MW01152230

The Best Kids Explore Vermont & The Adirondacks © 2022 by Joshua Best

Contact the publisher:
Unprecedented Press LLC - 229 W Main Ave, Zeeland, MI 49464
www.unprecedentedpress.com | info@unprecedentedpress.com
instagram: unprecedentedpress

ISBN: 978-1-7321964-9-0

Ingram Printing & Distribution, 2022

First Edition

the
BEST KIDS
explore

VERMONT
& THE ADIRONDACKS

An illustrated, story-driven travel guide for kids

CONTENTS

MEET THE KIDS 4

LODGING & TRANSPORT 6

STORIES:

LOG OFF 8
in Wilmington, NY

OUR SPRING 18
at Whiteface Mountain, NY

SWEET MEMORIES 26
in Waterbury, VT

HEAVEN'S CHEDDAR 36
in Shelburne, VT

LITTLE DETAILS 44

BEST BETS 45

BUMPS IN THE ROAD 46

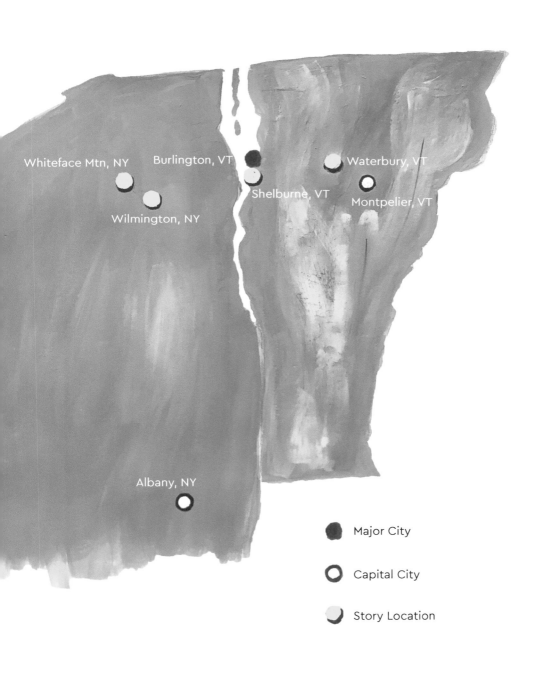

Whiteface Mtn, NY

Burlington, VT

Waterbury, VT

Wilmington, NY

Shelburne, VT

Montpelier, VT

Albany, NY

Major City

Capital City

Story Location

MEET THE KIDS

Exploring is the best. Exploring lets you discover the cool things around you – things you didn't know were there before. That's what makes it so much fun! It's exciting to find out what's around the corner, across the border and beyond the horizon.

The Best kids are explorers. They love finding new places to play and discovering new ways to have fun. The oldest is Frederick – he has orange hair. The middle child is Edith – she has brown hair. The youngest is Hugo – he has yellow hair. The Best kids are half American and half Canadian. They live in Michigan.

In this book, the kids travel to the states of Vermont and New York. At the time of their expedition, Frederick was six years old, Edith was four years old, and Hugo was one year old. This trip occurred in the month of May.

LODGING & TRANSPORT

The Best family travelled to Vermont and the Adirondack Mountains of New York by car. Specifically, they packed their gray Chevy Traverse chock-full of luggage in preparation for a five night stay in the mountains. Since they live in Michigan, they opted to travel across The Mitten State, over the Canadian border, through Ontario, and down into New York. They chose this route because it allowed them to stop and see their grandparents for a couple nights along the way. The kids' Nana and Papa live in central Ontario.

LOG CABIN AIRBNB

As you'll discover in the first story called *Log Off*, the best family booked an Airbnb for this trip. To match the setting, they found a cozy log cabin twenty miles east of Lake Placid, New York. The cabin slept seven people, so there was plenty of space to move around and be comfortable. The full kitchen allowed for healthy, affordable meals and the back deck offered a breathtaking view of the mountains. With rain in the forecast, this haven in the woods proved especially useful for spending an afternoon or two indoors.

LOG OFF

t was springtime, and the Best family had just sold their house. They were moving out of the suburbs, and into the walkable downtown area of a nearby town. It took them a little longer than they expected to find a new house, so they planned an epic road trip to help fill the time between homes.

The night before departing, they packed their bags with clothes, a couple books, and a few small toys for the journey. As they crawled into bed one final time in their old house, dad reminded them of the plan. The Best family reserved a log cabin in the Adirondack Mountains through Airbnb. Their plan was to stay for five nights and to explore the surrounging region.

It was 5:30 AM when they woke up and put their jackets on. The house was mostly empty because of the move, so they only needed to brush their teeth, get dressed, and file into the car. Their mom and dad were in the front seats, Hugo and Edith sat in the middle row, and Frederick sprawled out across the back with his art supplies and Rescue Bots. When the engine started, they rolled out of the driveway for one last time and waved goodbye to their old house in the suburbs. They were ready for a new place where they could be more connected to their neighbors.

The road to the Adirondacks had few stopovers. Because they were driving from Michigan and because the Great Lakes are so large, it was actually better for them to travel through Canada to get there. This worked out well for the Best kids because their Nana and Papa live in Ontario and they could stop in for a visit. When they arrived at Nana and Papa's house, they discovered that they had taken their dad to the Adirondacks many times when he was a kid, and they were happy the tradition was being passed on.

After a two-night stay, the kids got back on the road. By the time the kids arrived in the Adirondack Mountains, it was already getting late. They passed through Saranac

Lake, where they stopped for some groceries at the local Aldi. The sun disappeared from the horizon when they were loading groceries into the already-full trunk. As they got closer to their cabin in the Wilmington area, their mom (who was driving at the time) asked their dad about the details of their lodging arrangement.

"Do you have a key to get into the cabin?"

"Yes, of course!" Their dad replied. "The owner sent me a passcode to get in the front door. Let me find it."

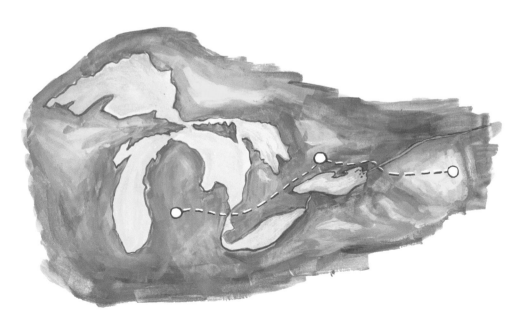

Dad picked up his phone, and opened the Airbnb app to find the message that contained the passcode.

"Uh oh..." A troubled look came over his face.

"What's wrong?" Hollered Frederick from the backseat.

"I don't have any reception on my phone. I can't access the message that has the passcode!"

Instantly, their plan to get off the grid for a few days was beginning to fall apart. Even their remote mountain getaway required a connection.

Together, they scrambled to make a new plan. With only a few minutes until they reached their destination, they decided to hunt for a coffee shop or restaurant with free Wi-Fi, so they could get the internet working again. As they pulled into the village of Wilmington, there was one church, one post office, one gas station and thankfully, one restaurant.

Mom swerved into the parking lot and the kids' dad jumped out of the car with his smartphone in hand. The next few minutes were quiet and tense. The kids were nervous they wouldn't have a place to sleep and their mom was frustrated. The sky had turned a shade of dark turquoise.

It took a little longer than expected, but their dad arrived back at the car with the passcode. The family-owned restaurant let him use their private Wi-Fi network to access the internet.

From the restaurant's location, it was only a few minutes up a steep side road and down a small laneway to the cabin. They parked the car in the driveway, and the team stretched, as they gathered their belongings. The kids lined up at the entrance with their bags, as their

dad typed in the passcode, which unlocked the door. The place was great – a perfect escape! It had a cozy living room with log walls of maple, a fireplace, and a large deck with Adirondack chairs overlooking the mountains. All of that was great, but there was one surprise feature that really excited them.

"Bunkbeds!" They cheered as they ran over to climb up on top. Frederick and Edith were thrilled to scale this impressive wooden structure, and instantly argued over who would sleep in the top bunk first. Hugo was

too young to sleep on the bunkbed, but he was thrilled that he got to sleep in the same room as his brother and sister for the first time ever. Once in bed, he kept them up late into the night because he couldn't stop talking.

The Best crew took it easy the next day. They cooked breakfast with supplies from the supermarket, they watched the movie *Smallfoot* together while snuggling on the couch, and their parents turned off their phones in exchange for reading books on the deck. In the evening, they stolled into the village for some grub.

Walking down the steep incline seemed challenging until the kids realized they would have to walk back up later, so they save the complaining for later. When the restaurant they visited the previous night was in view, they realized it was in a blue building with a small front porch made of wooden planks. On the porch, there was a statue of a bear that was carved out of wood and four metal letters that were installed on the outside wall. When they were still a couple hundred feet away, Frederick spelled out the word P-I-Z-Z-A.

About fifteen minutes later, they found themselves sitting quietly on the eatery's patio, gobbling hot pizza and coloring on napkins with crayons that were provided. They had a beautiful view of the river and the mountains. Their journey had just begun, but they already learned one important lesson: *It's healthy to get away, but everyone needs connection.* And sometimes, connection comes from the kindness of a hostess at a pizza place in the mountains.

They left a big tip.

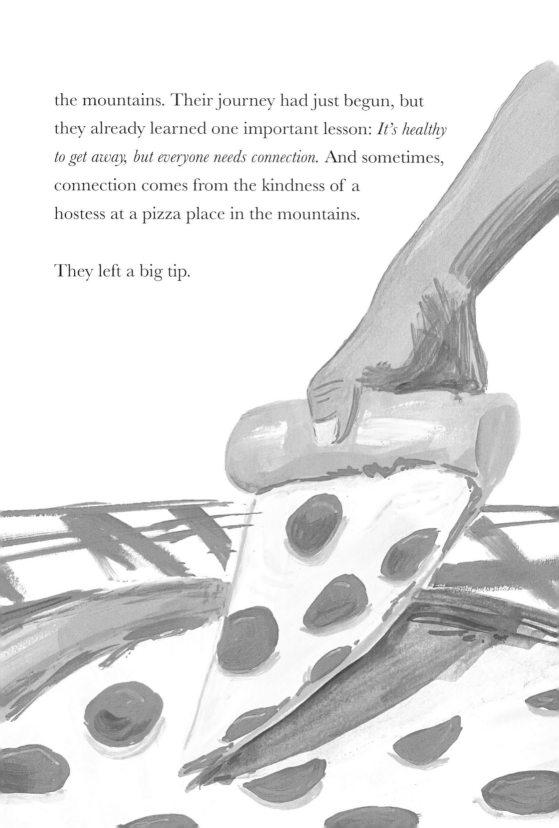

OUR SPRING

The Best kids' second full day in the Adirondacks was supposed to be filled with adventure, but instead it was filled with rain. Everything was wet. The grass, the deck, the Adirondack chairs, and yes, the fire pit. In the late afternoon, they tried to beat back the rain by making a fire anyways, but they didn't win. The rain won. And they went back inside.

On a positive note, the mountain rain felt fresh. It smelled good too. Actually, it was quite calming after a busy spring season to sit inside and hear the pitter-patter of raindrops on the roof. The kids' mom embraced the rain. She always finds joy in peaceful things. On the front lawn of the property, there was a flowering tree that looked

especially beautiful in the light of a sun shower, so she went outside to take pictures.

The next day, they were determined not to let the weather stop them from exploring, so they set off to visit Highfalls Gorge – a small river that pours down the mountain, and passes through a gully, which creates rapids and a waterfall. It was exciting to hear the loud roar of rushing water! After all, there was plenty of

it after yesterday's rainfall. The gorge had pathways, bridges and overlooks to improve your view. The guides had even compiled a scavenger hunt to help you spot natural features along the way.

HIGH FALLS GORGE

When the kids checked all the boxes on their scavenger list, they were given a free toy from the Visitor Center. They had so many fun options to choose from! Frederick found it hard to decide, but in the end chose a toy snake.

The family headed back to the cabin for lunch, and so that Hugo can take a nap. Luckily, the day of adventure wasn't over. After his nap, Hugo's dad put on his scary voice and asked, "Are you ready for Whiteface Mountain?"

Hugo's eyes got wide. He looked at his dad and replied, "My ready!"

The mountain (which was visible from the cabin), was only 10 minutes away, but the drive from the base to the summit took another 25 minutes. It didn't matter though – because the drive was stunning! They looped back-and-forth around hairpin curves and over cliff edges. They were ascending so high that their ears began to pop.

When they arrived at the summit parking lot, they zipped up their windbreakers and embarked on the foot path that would take them the rest of the way. It was much cooler on the mountaintop than it was in the valley. As they were walking, Frederick noticed a trickle of water dripping off the rockface beside him.

"Look, guys! a mountain spring! Can I drink some?"

His mom and dad look at each other. "Go for it, bud."

Frederick pressed his body up against the rock, crouched underneath the drip, opened his mouth, and stuck out his tongue.

"This is the best water I've ever tried!"

Frederick walked away with a big grin on his face – he was so proud of himself for discovering this natural source of refreshment.

The kids continued climbing, and got as high as they could, but had to stop at the second highest overlook because the path became too rugged for Hugo to climb in such windy conditions. They hung out at this perch for five or ten minutes, reveling in their accomplishment, and yet slightly disappointed they couldn't manage the last stretch.

Edith propped herself up on the rock ledge and peered out over the horizon. The layers of white clouds on the blue sky, and the layers of green trees over the brown earth seemed to go on for miles. The colors

lightened and faded into
the fog as the landscape
receded into the distance.

"It's really gorgeous!"
Edith observed.

The Best kids live in the Midwest, so they're not
used to observing so much of the world from such a
height. When you're so high up, you feel like you have
perspective. Not just on the area around you, but
perspective on life as well. That day, the Best family
reflected on the busy season they had left behind, and
became more excited about the fresh, spring season
ahead of them.

SWEET MEMORIES

On their fourth day exploring the region, the Bests wanted to wander a little further away from the cabin. They were headed for the great (but small) state of Vermont. It was Memorial Day weekend, and they wondered if some attractions might be a little busier, but it was still late spring (before most families start travelling), so they weren't terribly worried.

The only one of the bunch who had been to Vermont was the kids' dad. Their Nana and Papa took him to the Ben & Jerry's Ice Cream Factory when he was a kid. It was an experience that he cherished, and he told the kids how amazing it was. They were also getting excited to head down there and check it out!

The Ben & Jerry's Factory is located in a small Vermont town called Waterbury, which sits between Burlington (the largest city) and Montpelier (the capital city).

The trip to Waterbury wasn't exactly simple for the Bests. There were three legs to the journey. First, they had to conquer the eastern edge of the Adirondacks. Next, they had to drive their car onto a ferry boat and cruise across the impressive Lake Champlain. Lastly, they had to traverse the Green Mountains, which is the mountain range that Vermont is famous for (*if you know French, you'll recognize it in the name!*)

The first leg was twisty and turny with interesting homes and tiny villages around every corner. The second leg was more of a mental hurdle for the kids.

"We're driving the car onto a boat?" Questioned Hugo.

It seemed like a silly concept, but when there's a large body of water that separates two communities, a ferry is often more practical than a bridge. It's also much more fun! Once the car was parked on the boat, the kids were able to get out and climb up to the top deck.

The ride was absolutely breathtaking! The clear, crisp, blue water was rivaled only by the clear, crisp, blue sky.

Before the kids knew it, they were on dry ground, zooming past the city of Burlington and soaring through the Green Mountains. As she was taking in the scenery, the kids' mom remarked,

"Whoever chose the name for this mountain range picked the perfect one."

No one responded, but they all agreed. They were too mesmerized by the richness of the green grass and

the lush trees to take their eyes off the scenery outside their windows, or even to talk.

Toward the end of the third leg, Hugo had fallen asleep and the other two kids were getting anxious for ice cream. Their dad was excited to relive his childhood memory, but when they arrived they were surprised by how many cars were in the parking lot. The main parking area was completely full, so they drove to the overflow zone, but it was full too. Trying to make the best of it, they finally found a spot in the furthest lot. It was unpaved, with puddles everywhere.

As they approached the building, they noticed giant silos of cream, milk and sugar. The building was painted vibrant colors, and it was just the way their dad remembered! But when they turned the corner, they were confronted with an enormous line of people. There must've been 200 hungry customers waiting in line for ice cream! They tried to ignore the issue by approaching the special window for factory tours. The next tour was ten minutes away, which wasn't too bad. The facility smelled amazing and the painted murals in the waiting room were fun to look at, but it was hard to not be overwhelmed by the Memorial Day crowds.

On the tour, the kids watched a movie about the history of Ben & Jerry's and got to see how the ice cream is made. It was interesting, but it didn't quite live up to their dad's sales pitch. At the end of the tour, they each received a free sample of a new flavor with salted caramel. Everyone enjoyed it, except Frederick who offered his to Edith.

ON BEN & JERRY'S:
"I didn't like the free sample, but I loved the flavors we bought."

When they finished the tour, the line for the ice cream shop had not died down. In fact, it may have gotten longer! In an effort to salvage the experience, their dad suggested buying ice cream in a tub from the gift shop instead of cones from the window. Not a bad idea (in theory), but when they found a table, they had to share with another family because the rest of the seating was taken.

Dad headed inside to buy the pint-sized tubs, and emerged ten minutes later with three flavors. However, they didn't have any spoons at the gift shop, so he had to scramble back to find some. They had to wait a few more minutes, but then he returned victorious with spoons in hand! Finally, the kids dug into the delicious ice cream. Unfortunately, the ice cream that's sold in the gift shop is stored at "deep freeze" temperatures, so that it doesn't melt when you're driving home. The ice cream was so hard that the kids' spoons broke when they tried to take a bite. They had to wait another ten or fifteen minutes, before it was soft enough to scoop.

As they walked back to the car, the kids were (understandably) a little disappointed. To cheer them up, their dad encouraged them to check out the playground on the top of the hill. As they ran up to check it out, they discovered that most of the playground was barricaded off because it was being renovated.

The Best family collected themselves and got back on the road. They retraced their steps through the Green Mountains, were shuttled back across the shimmering waters of Lake Champlain, and weaved again through the twists and turns of the Adirondacks. Their experience at the ice cream factory may not have been as great as their dad remembered, but the trip was still fun! And with everyone's tummies filled with sugary goodness, they realized sometimes the journey is more enjoyable than the destination. And that's okay.

HEAVEN'S CHEDDAR

Most people have been to tourist attractions that are specifically designed for families – places like Disney World or Rainforest Cafe. But have you noticed there are some unique attrations that are just as suited for families, but far less manufactured? These places are more natural, and offer families a simpler, more authentic experience. Farmer's markets and National Parks would fit well in this category, and so would Vermont's Shelburne Farms on the eastern shores of Lake Champlain.

It was a sunny morning when the Best family arrived. Not knowing what to expect, they signed their names on a list for the next tractor ride that would take them over to the barn. But they wondered – will Hugo's stroller fit on a tractor ride? They waited just a few minutes in the warm sun and along came a big, green tractor pulling

a large, wooden wagon. As everyone climbed aboard, they realized it was spacious and well-built. No problem for a stroller!

The ride was delightful. Everyone was enjoying themselves – especially Edith who was simply beaming. She had really dressed for the occasion with her light sundress and yellow cardigan. She also brought a straw hat to keep her from getting burned. As they approach the end of the ride, Frederick spotted a gigantic fortress with a green roof and surrounded by a stone wall.

"Look at that castle!" He blurted out.

Edith and Hugo turned their heads to see. As they gawked at the incredible building, the wagon came to a stop in front of its gates. Frederick was very confused. "I thought we were going to a farm?"

His mom responded, "I think this is the barn."

"Cool!" Said Frederick.

"Cool!" Said Edith.

"Cool!" Said Hugo.

The Best kids jumped off the wagon and strolled up the laneway to the gates. Beyond the wall was a pastoral wonder – like something out of a dream. The rolling hills of green grass were dotted with picnic tables and featured a cute café serving gourmet sandwiches. Running around the lunch area were an equal number of chickens as children. These chickens were very

interested in our lunch, which sparked a nerve-wracking game of keep-away.

Off to the right of the grounds was a bakery serving cookies and fresh bread. To the left, a museum about farming. And in the far corner was something the kids couldn't resist; an adorable, young, dairy cow was brought out to interact with guests. Instantly, Edith and Frederick reached out their hands to touch the soft, white calf, and as they did, it turned its head and licked their hands.

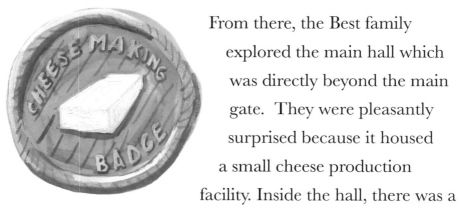

From there, the Best family explored the main hall which was directly beyond the main gate. They were pleasantly surprised because it housed a small cheese production facility. Inside the hall, there was a man with an apron, a mask and gloves, showing them how Vermont cheddar cheese is made. There was also a lady behind them with a tray of samples, which they gobbled down as they watched cheese being made from behind a window.

After visiting the cheese factory, the bakery, the museum and the café, the Best family sat down on the green grass, laid back and took a deep breath. With the sun on their faces, it felt like they were in heaven!

It was a perfectly peaceful moment, which was hilariously interrupted by another aggressive chicken looking for some leftovers. That was their signal to get back on the wagon, and wave goodbye to this pleasant wonderland called Shelburne Farms.

LITTLE DETAILS

WOODCARVINGS

In the Adirondack region of New York, the kids noticed an abundance of woodworking. As they drove through small towns and mountain villages, they spotted wooden statues of animals on display along the sides of the road. Hugo was especially fond of the wooden bear carving at the pizza joint in Wilmington.

THE GREENEST GRASS

After spending a few days in New York state, the Best kids traveled on a ferry across Lake Champlain and landed on the sunny shores of Vermont. The deeper they went into the interior of the state, the greener and more lush the scenery became. It was immediately apparent why Vermont is referred to as the "Green Mountain State." It was by far the greenest green they had ever seen.

BEST BETS

SHELBURNE FARMS

The story about Shelburne Farms raves about its beauty in abundance, so it we won't elaborate too much here. Just go on a sunny day, and you won't be disappointed.

 ★★★★ ★★★★½ ★★★★★

WHITEFACE MOUNTAIN

The winding road up to Whiteface Mountain was fun for the kids, and so was the footpath. Additionally, there's a small castle-looking structure near the summit with a cafe and a gift shop. It's a nice, little milestone on your way up the mountain.

 ★★★★★ ★★★★  ★★★★★

BUMPS IN THE ROAD

ELBOW INJURY

At High Falls Gorge, the kids were able to run and climb on rock and logs. At one point, Frederick asked his dad to record a slow-motion video of him jumping off a boulder that was beside the path. Unfortunately, he caught his elbow on the edge as he jumped, and now we have a slo-mo video of his injury.

WI-FI SIGNAL

As mentioned in *Log Off*, the kids' dad made the mistake of not capturing the passcode to the cabin beforehand. When they tried to "log on" to get the code, there was no reception. We definitely recommend taking a screenshot of any cloud-based details before visiting mountainous areas.

WIND & RAIN

Depending on the time of year you travel, note that the mountains of New England and New York can get chilly. On Whiteface Mountain the winds were very strong, and we had at least two days of rain, which is expected when travelling in May.

DEEP FREEZE ICE CREAM

As mentioned in *Sweet Memories*, the lines at Ben & Jerry's were very long, so we opted for pre-packaged ice cream from the gift shop. We didn't realize it was frozen to an extreme degree for extended travel.

ANGRY CHICKENS

The funniest *bump in the road* on this trip was the chicken encounter at Shelburne Farms. They were pretty aggressive, and yet super entertaining. Despite the nerves, it was a good experience for non-farm kids.

ABOUT THE
AUTHOR

The adventures of the Best kids found on these pages
were chronicled by none other than their own father.
Joshua Best is a writer, designer, and illustrator. By day,
he leads the marketing team at a nonprofit network
of children's hospitals. Of all these roles, there is none
better than being a dad to Frederick, Edith and Hugo.

FOLLOW
ALONG

Why wait until the next book is released when you can find out now where the kids are headed next? Follow the kids on Instagram to watch illustration in progress and to see real photos of current trips! Also, check out the website for ways to get in touch.

 @thebestkidsexplore

 thebestkidsexplore.com